P. Doolan

IRELAND

from old photographs

1. (*overleaf*) The Donnybrook Tram (*A. V. Henry*)

IRELAND

from old photographs

Introduction and commentaries by

MAURICE GORHAM

B. T. BATSFORD LTD
LONDON

B. T. Batsford Limited,
4 Fitzhardinge St, London W1
Printed and bound in Great Britain by
Jarrold & Sons Limited, Norwich, Norfolk
First published 1971
7134 0115 X

*To my sister
Nora Bartels
for her advice and help*

CONTENTS

INTRODUCTION

The Victorian epoch was not a happy time for Ireland. It saw the Famine, when starvation and emigration carried off two million people within a few years; two abortive insurrections, savagely suppressed; the Land War, with its evictions and boycotts; the sensational Park Murders, followed by the equally sensational fall of Parnell.

If Edwardian times bore a more peaceful air, with Irish national aspirations seemingly crystallised round the Parliamentary struggle for Home Rule, there was still emigration from the countryside, misery in the towns, and the smoulderings beneath the surface that were to erupt in violence in 1913 and 1916.

Little of this was recorded by the camera. Photographers of the period were mainly occupied with the domestic scene and the commercial round of portraits and postcard views, varied by royal processions and other formal occasions. It was exceptional for the harsher side of life to find its way into the lens.

So this does not profess to be a pictorial history. For that one would have to use the engravings that appeared so profusely in, for instance, the *Illustrated London-News*. Evictions, processions, riots and all such events were depicted in vivid detail, but seldom by men who had seen them happening. Up to the time when the half-tone process came in and made direct reproduction of photographs in newspapers possible, even photographs taken on the spot were copied by artists for engraving, and authenticity could vanish in the process.

Of course photographs are not necessarily true to fact either – we have learnt a lot about how the camera can be made to lie – but except for one or two that are included as interesting fakes, we think it can be claimed that the photographs in this book show what they purport to show. What they give us is a panorama of life in Ireland – the life that many people lived from the 1840s to the first decade of this century, with undue emphasis certainly on the sunny side, but with an occasional glimpse of what was going on underneath.

That has been the aim throughout: to show people in their surroundings, as the best way of illustrating what life was like in Ireland in the past. For this reason straightforward portraits have been avoided, for the most part, and photographs of scenes and buildings without people. Sometimes it has been possible to identify individuals; more often not. But these are our ancestors, and this is what they looked like in their time.

Photography came early to Ireland. It was in 1839 that Daguerre launched his invention in France and W. H. Fox Talbot revealed his to the Royal Society in London, and by 1842 a daguerrotype studio had been set up in Dublin: the Daguerrotype Portrait Insitution in Sackville Street (now O'Connell Street), run by a Hungarian, 'Professor' Gluckman. The craze for having one's likeness 'drawn by the camera' caught on; in 1847, for instance, a daguerrotype artist was touring the country towns offering portraits on silver plate, very much like the 'sticky-backs' still being taken by itinerant photographers a hundred years later, only these were sold for 12s 6d a time.

Before that, when Daniel O'Connell was sent to jail after the banning of his monster meeting at Clontarf in 1843, the daguerrotype found its way even there. As Charles Gavan Duffy recorded in his book *Young Ireland*,

> 'An artist's studio and a daguerrotypist's camera were set up within the precincts to multiply likenesses of the prisoners, and the caricaturists made more amusing ones without the trouble of a sitting.'

Multiplying the likenesses was done by making lithographed copies, not only of the prisoners but of their friends who visited them in jail; many such portraits appeared in T. F. Sullivan's book *The Young Irelanders* and single portraits found a ready sale all over the country.

This sounds like an easy-going form of imprisonment, and so it was. The Liberator was sent to the Richmond Bridewell, which was owned by Dublin Corporation; the Governor gave up his own house to his guest, and O'Connell entertained his supporters by the score. But when the Young Irelanders themselves were imprisoned after the failure of the rising of 1848 they were sent to Kilmainham Jail. This was a very different proposition; yet the daguerrotypist found his way there too, as witness the picture of William Smith O'Brien and T. F. Meagher with their jailers (161). This, by the way, is one of the few portrait groups, as opposed to single portraits, taken in Ireland at the time.

Photography soon became a hobby, not to say an art, as well as a trade. Fox Talbot himself visited Ireland and left some records of his stay (for examples see 3, 4, 196, 197). In 1854 the first photographic society was founded – the Dublin Photographic Society, with Lord Otho FitzGerald as its first chairman. Its foundation date was November 8, 1854, which makes it the second oldest national photographic society in the world: the Royal Photographic Society in London was founded a year earlier and the French Photographic Society a week later. It changed its name to the Photographic Society of Ireland in 1858, and it is still going strong.

The Society continued to encourage progress in the art and science of photography and among its records are famous names such as those of John Shaw Smith, who took the first photographs of the city of Petra; Professor John Joly, F.R.S., of Trinity College, Dublin, the pioneer of colour photography; Professor J. Alfred Scott, Alfred Werner, and Thomas H. Mason, author-illustrator of *The Islands of Ireland*. Its fixtures included, in 1890, Professor Muybridge's lecture on 'Animal Locomotion', illustrated by his series of photographs of a horse in action, which not only corrected previous ideas of how a horse gallops (including those of innumerable artists), but led directly to the invention of cinematography.

There must have been a lot of ardent amateurs taking photographs all over Ireland for the Society's annual competitions, but so far as the commercial photographers were concerned, their work was mainly in two categories – studio portraits and views that could be made into postcards for sale. The greatest of them was William Lawrence, who started a photographer's business in association with his toyshop in Upper Sackville Street, Dublin, in the 1870s and made it into a very flourishing concern. Photography was far from being his sole interest. His entry in Thom's Directory at the turn of the century read as follows:

Sackville Street, Upper
5, 6, 7 – Lawrence, Wm. photographer, printseller, framemaker, artists' colourman, toy and fancy merchants, cricketing and tennis outfitters, Irish bog oak carvers, and jewellers.

But his photographs have survived when his toys and bog oak carvings have long disappeared. They survived the destruction of so much of Dublin at Easter 1916, at least his landscapes and street scenes did, though his portrait negatives were destroyed. The collection remained intact until his own death in 1932, at the age of 91, and for another ten years. Then by great good fortune it was bought by the National Library in Dublin: 40,000 plates bought for £300 – an average of $1\frac{3}{4}$d a plate.

This was a rare piece of luck – rare especially in Ireland, where so many collections have been lost or destroyed. Lawrence's chief photographer, Robert French, had travelled all over Ireland – undivided then – photographing towns, villages, country scenes, and sometimes family houses and groups. His pictures formed the basis of innumerable postcards and of those oblong photographs in railway carriages, always a decade or two behind the times – ladies in sweeping skirts and spreading hats in days when skirts were short and the cloche hat was supreme

– that added charm to railway journeys between the wars.

The Lawrence Collection is well used; recently more than one book has been compiled entirely from it, and an excellent short film on James Joyce's Dublin used only Lawrence photographs. This in spite of the conditions under which the plates are kept. The National Library accomplished a coup by buying them, but owing to shortage of staff, space and money it has not been able to make access to them easy. There is no set of prints: the seeker has to view the negatives one by one, holding up the glass plate against the light – not the most convenient way for him, and one fraught with danger to the plate.

The collection has its limitations, including the fact that a large proportion of the photographs are static – pictures of places with no living thing in sight. This was not unnatural, considering the purpose for which they were taken. Robert French could make live enough photographs when he wanted to – witness his street scenes full of traffic, and fair day scenes crowded with men and beasts; but when the object is to get pictures of buildings or scenery, people are apt to be a nuisance. They move about, they pose for the camera, their clothes date. Photographs of resorts have to have them – there is no allure in an empty promenade; but plates that would make good postcards were often best taken with a small aperture and long exposure. If the exposure was long enough, anybody who came on the scene would pass across without registering on the plate. The result is that many of his photographs, though excellent in detail, give us little or no sense of period; and there is something uncanny about a photograph of Eyre Square, Galway, for instance, with nobody about.

Nor can there have been much incentive to take photographs of events that would not make saleable postcards. Evictions were being carried out by the hundred in the years when Robert French was touring Ireland, but it is only occasionally that we find photographs of them, such as those reproduced in nos. 162-5.

This latter limitation was not confined to the Lawrence Collection. Irish photographers were slow to turn their attention to the seamy side. All through the Edwardian period they tended to concentrate on the official occasion and ignore the unseemly; we get pictures of royal processions with street decorations, plumed hats and glittering escorts, rather than of hostile demonstrations and other breaches of the peace. One of the classic news photographs is the one taken by Joseph Cashman of police batoning the crowds in Sackville Street – but that was not until 1913.

However, the Lawrence Collection remains the chief source of photographs for the period from 1880 to 1910, and it is indeed fortunate that it has survived. There are smaller collections in museums and libraries, notably in Belfast, and some pockets of photographs of Irish interest in the Victoria and Albert Museum and the Science Museum in London, and some of them go back to the period before Lawrence began. But all too often collections have disappeared. Lafayette and Chancellor, two great Dublin photographers – their collections vanished when the firms changed hands. T. H. Mason's stock was destroyed only a few years ago, in a disastrous fire, and only scattered prints and slides remain. Valuable photographs disappeared in diverse ways. Plates were washed to provide glass for picture-frames and even for greenhouses; nobody knows how many photographs of interest were on plates that were sold for the value of the glass during the 1914-18 war.

Fate seems to have been especially unkind to Irish photographic history. Everywhere one looks one finds that private collections have been mislaid, or thrown out as rubbish, some only a year or two ago. All the more reason to be thankful for those that have survived, such as those that grace the walls in the Dublin clubhouse of the century-old Wanderers Football Club or those that the Stevens Cycle Company brought with it to Bachelor's Walk when it crossed the river from Aston's Quay.

So getting this book together has been a matter of tapping many sources and following up many clues. My own family albums yielded one or two photographs but not many; our ancestors were apt to think of photography as something to be practised in distant parts, and they brought back pictures of the Far East but took few in Connemara when they got home. But I have had help from the most diverse quarters; none of the many people I approached was unwilling to help.

Sometimes the help took the form of telling me of people who might have photographs, who proved to have none but who knew other people who might have photographs, who also proved to have none. But then there were the people who revealed unsuspected hoards; people who cut up family albums and lent me irreplaceable prints; who produced boxes of negatives found in other people's lumber-rooms, or bought at auctions for the sake of the box without knowning that there were negatives inside.

There is another difficulty – dates. The Lawrence plates name the place where the photograph was taken (though even this is not invariably correct) but not the date, and the numbers on the plates are no sure guide. As for the pictures from private sources, many have neither place nor date. Sometimes it is possible to deduce one or the other, and this is easiest when transport enters into the picture.

The transport experts can look at a picture showing a tram, for instance, and tell exactly when that type came into service and when it went out.

Sometimes clothes help in dating, sometimes buildings, but in pictures of country towns and scenes there was often little change in the surroundings from one generation to the next. Nor did country people always follow the fashions; clothes that looked as if they might belong to the 1860s were still being worn in some places up to comparatively recent times.

There are photographs here that have no history; nobody knows who took them and how many hands they went through. These are the hardest to place or date; sometimes one can make a guess, but some of the guesses may be wildly wrong. So indeed may some of the attributions that we think are fairly certain; somebody will always know better. But we think we have kept fairly closely to our original aim – to make our panorama run from the beginnings of photography to the end of the Edwardian era. Now and again we have gone over that limit by a year or two, but we think that very few of these photographs could have been taken much later than 1910.

We, in this connection, means myself and Sam Carr of Batsfords, who did all the collecting in London and Belfast. In addition, he took his full share in the most trying part of the process – the final selection, when we had to decide which of the stacks of pictures we had collected could not be got into the book.

Among those to whom special thanks are due for their help either in finding photographs or in placing and dating them are Douglas Bennett, Desmond Clarke, Librarian of the Royal Dublin Society, F. E. Dixon, Dr Patrick Flanagan, A. V. Henry, and Mrs William Jameson (Flora Mitchell, the painter).

Also to S. Bohan, Cork City Librarian; Mary Collins and Anthony Barry; Robert C. Booth and Michael E. Booth; Frank Burke, Sean Dowling, Conor McGinley, and Colm O Lochlainn; Liam Byrne, of the National Library, Dublin; Joseph Cashman; Captain Kevin Danaher; Professor J. H. Delargy, Director of the Irish Folklore Commission; Father Thomas Egan, of Ballintubber Abbey, and Desmond Wynne; Dermot Foley, of the Libary Council; G. S. Forde, of Wanderers F.C.; Edward I. Gibson; Major R. D. Greer, of the Royal Irish Automobile Club; Professor Denis Gwynn and Mrs T. G. Moorhead; Dr Richard Hayes; G. A. Henry; Dr. J. de Courcy Ireland, of the Maritime Institute of Ireland; C. Gordon Lambert, of Irish Biscuits Ltd.; and Una Cunnane; Tom Lambert and Dr H. S. Corran, of Arthur Guinness Son and Co. Ltd.; Oscar S. Merne, Phyllis Thompson, and Elizabeth Duffy, of the Photographic Society of Ireland; Niall Montgomery;

Professor T. W. Moody, F.T.C.D.; Fr. Moroney of Dun Laoghaire; George Morrison; Alan Newham; Fachtna Ó hAnnracháin; Phil O'Kelly and Maura Woods, of the Abbey Theatre; Pádraic Ó Raghallaigh; Frank O'Reilly, Kevin C. McCourt, Aleck Crichton, and Mrs Pat Wilson, of United Distillers of Ireland Ltd.; Seán Ó Síocháin, of the Gaelic Athletic Association; and J. F. Burke, of the *Midland Tribune*; Sean O Súilleabháin; Mary Purcell, of the National Monuments Branch, Office of Public Works; Jim Robson; D. E. Stevens, of Stevens Cycle Company; Maura Tallon, of the Civic Museum, Dublin; and Harold White.

Finally to Mrs Eleanor Wiltshire of Green Studio and Richard Deegan of Deegan-Photo, experts at printing and copying, who could be relied upon to produce good prints from time-worn originals and to safeguard irreplaceable negatives and prints.

IN THE CITIES

2. Seen on the streets of Dublin at the turn of the century (*A. V. Henry*)

3. Fox Talbot in Dublin: W. H. Fox Talbot, the pioneer of photography, left a few photographs taken in Ireland, marked with his strong sense of composition. This photograph of St. George's church, Hardwicke Place, Dublin, was taken in 1845. The church, one of the finest buildings of Francis Johnston, dates from 1802–13 (*Science Museum*)

4. (*opposite*) The Castle Guard in the 1840s – another Fox Talbot study. In the background is the Bedford Tower over the Office of Heralds, now the Genealogical Office (*B. T. Batsford*)

5. Carlisle Bridge and Sackville Street in 1864; the trams had not yet come into the picture and there are no statues between the bridge and the Pillar (*Radio Times/Hulton*)

6. The next stage – the horse trams, started in 1875, have left their tracks all over the picture. The statue is of Sir John Gray, proprietor of the *Freeman's Journal,* Member of Parliament, and father of Dublin's water supply. On the left is the portico of the General Post Office, one of Dublin's most historic buildings, and in the background is the Nelson Pillar, which was blown up in 1966 (*Frith & Co*)

7. Early Twentieth Century: the trams have gone electric, the massive monument to Daniel O'Connell the Liberator has risen at the foot of what has become O'Connell Bridge. The towering building on the right, owned by the Dublin Bread Company, figured prominently in the Easter Rising of 1916 (*National Library, Dublin*)

8. (*opposite above*) Old Essex Bridge, linking Capel Street and Parliament Street, with the Four Courts in the distance, and the Presbyterian church, since demolished, on Ormond Quay. The bridge was rebuilt in 1874 (*Royal Dublin Society*)

9. (*opposite below*) Old Carlisle Bridge in 1877 – hump-backed, with no middle island (*Royal Dublin Society*)

10. (*below*) O'Connell Bridge, seen here about 1902. Since then the trams and sidecars have gone, the statue of William Smith O'Brien has been moved across the river, the Carlisle Building on the left-hand corner has gone, but the turreted building opposite, at the corner of D'Olier Street and Westmoreland Street, remains (*National Library, Dublin*)

11. The Castle Guard of a later generation than Fox Talbot's – some of them keenly conscious of the camera, as is the boy standing in the gateway to Upper Castle Yard (*National Library*)

12. When the Union Jack flew over the Viceregal Lodge in Phoenix Park — now Arus an Uachtarain, the official residence of the President of Ireland (*Radio Times/Hulton*)

13. (*overleaf*) A sleepy scene outside Leinster House, built as the town house of the FitzGeralds, later the home of the Royal Dublin Society from 1814 to 1924 and the scene of the first Dublin Horse Shows. It is now the Parliament House of Ireland. On the right is the National Museum, built in 1890 (*National Library*)

14: Grafton Street in the 1890s, with the railings of the Provost's House of Trinity College on the right, the main facade of Trinity at the foot, and the East colonnade of the Bank of Ireland beyond (*Radio Times/Hulton*)

15. Grafton Street, here seen from nearer St Stephen's Green, still sees smart pair-horse turn-outs, but behind them is an ominous newcomer – the motor car. The shop at the corner of Suffolk Street, on the left, then Jaeger, has been occupied by Weir's the silversmiths since 1910 (*National Library*)

16. The children are grouped round the base of one of Dublin's finest monuments – John Van Nost's statue of George II in St Stephen's Green. Like most royal statues in Dublin, it has long since been destroyed (*A. V. Henry*)

17, 18. Bill-sticking was widespread and promiscuous. Evocative are the cheap fares to Drogheda (*below*) and the Royal Irish Constabulary sports at Ballsbridge (*right*) (*17, National Library; 18, A. V. Henry*)

19, 20. In the Liberties – one of the oldest (and once the poorest) parts of Dublin – New Row and Blackpitts, in the shadow of St Patrick's Cathedral (*National Library*)

21. There is hardly a street or building in the Dublin of 1904 that does not figure in the writings of James Joyce, but the best-known pub scene in *Ulysses* is set in Barney Kiernan's pub, which Bloom left on the sidecar pursued by the Citizen's dog. The pub's position in Little Britain Street, close to the Four Courts, accounted for the title 'The Court of Appeal' (*A. V. Henry*)

22. The Market on the Stones in Patrick Street, Dublin, close to St. Patrick's Cathedral – clearing up after snow (*A. V. Henry*)

23. Peter Street in 1894: the buildings shown here were shortly to be demolished to make way for a new building for Jacob's, the famous Dublin biscuit factory (*W. & R. Jacob & Co. Ltd*)

24. Belfast in the late Nineties – Castle Place, at the corner of Royal Avenue (*Ulster Museum*)

25. The Linen Hall, Belfast, in the 1880s. Built in 1785, it was demolished in 1898 to make room for the new City Hall (*Ulster Museum/R. J. Welch*)

26. (*opposite*) Building Belfast's City Hall. The decorations are in honour of a royal visit in July 1903 (*Linen Hall Library*)

27. (*overleaf*) Donegall Place, Belfast, in the 1880s, with Anderson and McCauley's premises on the right (still there in 1970) and the Linen Hall in the distance (*National Library*)

28. Schooners discharging coal at Queen's Quay, Belfast, in 1880 (*London Library*)

29. Catastrophe in the Eighties: spectators viewing the remains of the Albert Bridge, Belfast, after the collapse of the central arches in 1886 (though some of them can't resist the lure of the camera) (*Ulster Museum/R. J. Welch*)

30. Castle Place, Belfast, again – in the 1880s. The horse trams survived in Belfast until 1904 (*Ulster Museum/R. J. Welch*)

31. Donegall Place again, in 1888, just after Robinson and Cleaver completed their Linen Warehouse, seen on the right. The photograph was taken from in front of the old Linen Hall (*Ulster Museum/R. J. Welch*)

32. The Royal Alhambra Theatre of Varieties, Belfast, in April 1911. For 4d or 6d one could see
a bill including the Filmograph (*Ulster Museum/R. J. Welch*)

33. On the Quay at Cork; a photograph taken by William England in 1859
(*Radio Times/Hulton*)

34. The South Mall, Cork at the corner of Morrison's Island, about 1875 (*Radio Times/Hulton*)

35. Patrick's Quay, Cork, with the paddle-steamer *Albert* about to pass under the bridge built in 1911 (*National Library*)

36. Patrick Street, Cork, in the 1890s: The 'Keep Left' sign seems to be an example of traffic control running ahead of traffic (*Radio Times/Hulton*)

37. The Victoria Hotel, Cork, in 1898 (it is still there in 1970) with the hotel bus at the door and sidecars in attendance. The standard for the electric trams is already in position, waiting for the wires (*National Library*)

38. 'The Statue', still a Cork landmark as it was when the photograph was taken in 1900. It honours Father Mathew, the apostle of Total Abstinence in the first half of the Nineteenth Century (*National Library*)

39. Reginald's Tower, the best-known building in Waterford, and the Quay, as it was about 1895 (*Belfast Central Library*)

40. The Mall, Waterford, decorated for the visit of Edward VII in 1903 – but with troops more in evidence than crowds (*National Library*)

41. Eyre Square, Galway, in the 1890s: a welter of carts and cattle between the Bank of Ireland (in the background) and the Salthill tram, waiting to bring its passengers to the seaside (*National Library*)

42. George's Street, Limerick. It is now O'Connell Street, but Cruise's Hotel, on the left, is still there (*Radio Times/Hulton*)

43. Waterloo Place, Derry – a view from Guildhall Square looking down to Strand Road, with horse-trams, the ubiquitous sidecar and the porch of the old Northern Counties Hotel halfway down on the right (*Ulster Museum*)

44. How an older woman should dress – in Co. Limerick in 1905 (*Kevin Danaher*)

ON THE ROAD

45. The Galway-Clifden mail car ready to leave: one of the famous Bianconi cars, named after Carlo Bianconi, the Italian print-seller who founded Ireland's most efficient road transport system. His Galway-Clifden service began in 1837, one car each way every day, and ran until the railway opened in 1895 – long after Bianconi himself had sold out and died. When this photograph was taken, in the early 1880s, the fare for the 49 miles was 7s 6d, plus 'whip money' to the driver (*National Library*)

46. A sedate family party outside the Grosvenor Hall, Rathmines (*Dr W. E. Boles*)

47. By wagonette from Malahide Castle (*Mrs Wm. Jameson*)

48. Connemara tandem: Dr Pitt Gorham, of Clifden, Co. Galway, in his tandem, with his sister behind and his lady cousin holding the reins. Standing in the centre is another cousin, Matt Coneys, afterwards well known in the New York Harbour Customs. The house in the background is now a guest-house

49. Round the Lakes by sidecar – or jaunting-car, as it is sometimes called (*National Library*)

50. The Glengarriff tourist coach ran from Macroom, where the railway ended, to Gougane Barra and Glengarriff, Co. Cork. Here it is in the 1890s, pulled up in front of the premises of 'Jeremiah Sullivan, licensed to sell beer, spirits & wine by retail' (*National Library*)

51. By coach to Shanganagh, from the Shelbourne Hotel in St. Stephen's Green, about 1899. The first coach is driven by Mr Kitt Malcolmson, the second, with a team of greys, by Sir James Power, of the famous Dublin distillers (*United Distillers of Ireland Ltd*)

52. Tourist coaches ran from McNeill's hotel at Larne to the Giant's Causeway from 1853. This one was photographed at Garron Point on the Antrim Coast Road, about 1907 (*National Library*)

53. Three wheels are safer than two – a peaceful scene in Phoenix Park (*National Library*)

54. Cyclist's rest at Kilmacanogue in the Wicklow Mountains; outside the Post Office in 1896 (*A. V. Henry*)

55. The tallest bicycle in Ireland – made by Stevens Cycle Company for Maurice Woolfe, of the Dublin Metropolitan Police, who stood 6,ft 8 ins and weighed 21 stone. This photograph, which hangs in Dublin Civic Museum, was taken around the turn of the century, but Maurice Woolfe (seen up) was a familiar figure around Dublin even after the D.M.P. was abolished, as a separate force, in 1925 (*Civic Museum/Stevens Cycle Manufacturers*)

56. In the heyday of the bicycle – the Stevens Quint of 1900: a five-man team of racing experts, with R. W. Stevens himself in the lead (*Stevens Cycle Manufacturers*)

57. The next stage – the motor-tricycle. The setting of this picture appears to be Trinity College, Dublin, but the identity of the rider has not been traced (*Stevens Cycle Manufacturers*)

58. Enter the motorcar: a party from Glasgow at Tunnel Cottage, Glengarriff, Co. Cork, in the days when veils and goggles were useful equipment for a country drive (*National Library*)

59. (*overleaf*) At the Windy Gap, Co. Kerry, about 1910: private motorists and char-a-bancs on the 'Grand Atlantic' tour by Parknasilla, Waterville and Cahirciveen (*National Library*)

60. Touring in Co. Donegal: visitors from London at Duntally, Creeslough, about 1907 (*National Library*)

61. The owner at the wheel, the chauffeur by his side. The car was the first to be registered in Co. Leitrim under the Motor Car Act of 1903; the photograph was taken outside the Spa Hotel at Lucan, Co. Dublin (*National Library*)

62, 63. Motor char-a-bancs, run by the railway, toured Connemara from 1911 on. Here they are in Clifden (*above*), outside the Railway Hotel (now the Clifden Bay Hotel), with the Catholic church in the background; and (*below*) at McKeown's Hotel in Leenane, now the Leenane Hotel (*National Library*)

64. (*overleaf*) Off to the Cork Exhibition in 1902; Sir Thomas Power, of the famous Dublin distillers, at the wheel, with the chauffeur beside him; Lady Power in the back, with Mr and Mrs J. R. O'Reilly. The primitive-looking car carried them safely from Mount Merrion House near Dublin to Cork (*United Distillers of Ireland Ltd.*)

ROUND THE COUNTRY

66. Going for the turf in Co. Sligo, about 1900 (*Ulster Museum/R. J. Welch*)

65. (*opposite*) The old Kerryman – one of Robert French's studies of a timeless country type (*National Library*)

67. In the heart of the mountains: a cottage in the Gap of Dunloe, in Co. Kerry (*F. E. Dixon*)

68. A primitive form of haulage in Glenshesk, Ballycastle, Co. Antrim – solid wheels on the farm car (*Ulster Museum/R. J. Welch*)

69. Corpus Christi: a procession passing through Athea, Co. Limerick, about 1910 (*Kevin Danaher*)

70. Stampy Party, Co. Limerick, 1907–8: 'stampy' was made from grated raw potatoes, flour and seasoning. The party was given, at the end of the potato harvest, by the farmer to workers, neighbours and helpers (*Kevin Danaher*)

71. Castlebar, Co. Mayo, in the early Eighties; everybody looking at the camera, which is outside the gates of the Cavalry Barracks (*Victoria and Albert Museum*)

72. Perfect peace at Roundwood, Co. Wicklow, with two smartly-dressed men posing on the sidecar – driven, apparently, by a boy (*Radio Times/Hulton*)

73. Coming from Mass: the congregation outside the Church of the Sacred Heart, Roscommon – or 'the chapel' as Catholic churches were often called, whatever their size, when 'church' implied a building of the Church of Ireland (*National Library*)

74. Getting ready to spin on the old wheel outside a cottage at Bushmills, Co. Antrim (*Ulster Museum*)

75. Fair Day in the Square, Listowel, Co. Kerry (*National Library*)

76. Puck Fair in Killorglin, Co. Kerry, with the mountain goat enthroned for the three days of the fair. The custom is kept up to this day (*National Library*)

Fair Day was the great day in Irish country towns, north and south – the day for meeting friends as well as doing business

77-80. Here are fair day scenes in Armagh (*opposite, top*), Carrickmacross, Co. Monaghan (*opposite, below*), Roscommon (*above*), and Bantry, Co. Cork (*below*) (*National Library*)

81. A different sort of fair: geese on display in Dundalk, Co. Louth (*National Library*)

AMONG THE RUINS

82. Antiquaries of the Sixties in the ruins of Kilcrea Abbey' – a Franciscan friary of 1465, near Ballincollig, Co. Cork. Photographed by William England (*Radio Times/Hulton*)

83. On a cromlech near Castlewellan, Co. Down: however elaborate their dress, Victorian ladies were capable of great feats for the photographer. This picture, from the Annesley family album, was taken at Legananny on the Annesley estate about 1895 (*Public Record Office of N. I.*)

84. Stopping to say a prayer at St. Finbarr's Oratory, Gougane Barra, Co. Cork, where the saint had an island hermitage (*National Library*)

85. Monasterboice, Co. Louth, a monastic settlement dating at least from the 8th century. This photograph shows the Round Tower and Muireadach's Cross in 1875, when work was beginning on clearing up the site (*National Monuments Branch, Office of Public Works*)

86. Muireadach's Cross again – one of the finest High Crosses in Ireland –
with two visitors from the Sixties or Seventies (*C. Flewitt*)

87. Relaxing among the ruins (*National Monuments Branch*)

88. Glendalough in the 1850s: the ruins of the settlement that grew up around St. Kevin's hermitage, in the most beautiful part of Co. Wicklow, attract thousands of visitors today (*F. E. Dixon*)

THE ISLANDS

89. Life on the islands round the coasts of Ireland changed little over the years. Some of them have now been abandoned by their inhabitants, but not the Aran Islands, the Irish-speaking islands in Galway Bay. This photograph, showing islanders on the road to the steamer on Inishmore, the largest of the islands, was taken by Thomas H. Mason, the photographer and author of *The Islands of Ireland* (*T. H. Mason*)

90. Women coming from Mass on Inishmaan, another of the Aran Islands (*T. H. Mason*)

91. Waiting for the steamer on the strand at Inishmaan, Aran Islands. (*T. H. Mason*)

92. (*opposite*) In the ruined Church of the Four Comely Saints on Arranmore, three miles from the coast of Co. Donegal (*Ulster Museum /R. J. Welch*)

93. On Tory Island, Co. Donegal, in 1895 – an isolated community with a primitive way of life (*Belfast Central Library*)

94. A desolate scene in West Town, Tory Island (*Ulster Museum/R. J. Welch*)

95. Inside a cottage on the Blasket Islands, off the coast of Co. Kerry: the woman of the house at her spinning-wheel (*T. H. Mason*)

96. In the village of Duagh, on Achill Island, Co. Mayo (*Radio Times/Hulton*)

97. Rathlin Island, six miles off Ballycastle, at the northern tip of Co. Antrim. The landmark on the far side is described merely as 'Mr. Gage's House' (*Ulster Museum/R. J. Welch*)

98. Fish curing on Clare Island, Co. Mayo; across the water, 'Granuaile's Castle', called after Grace O'Malley, the sea-queen of the West in the sixteenth century, who had her stronghold here (*National Library*)

ON THE WATER

99. (*previous page*) A peaceful outing on Muckross Lake, Killarney, in the 1870s (*Victoria and Albert Museum*)

100. (*above*) A Bray boatman – P. Cranley with his boat *Alice*

101. (*opposite, above*) Currachs at Rosapenna, Co. Donegal. These frail-looking boats, made of tarred canvas stretched over a frame of laths, are able to ride the Atlantic waves all down the West coast of Ireland (*Ulster Museum/R. J. Welch*)

102. (*opposite, below*) Round coracles on the Boyne, a more primitive type of craft. Both currachs and coracles originally had coverings of hide (*T. H. Mason*)

103. Ships of war in Killary Bay: this deep inlet of the Atlantic, between Galway and Mayo, could take the biggest ships of the nineteenth century. Here is the Channel Squadron steaming up the bay on its visit in October 1899 (*National Library*)

104. (*opposite, above*) Queenstown (now Cobh) Harbour, about 1870, with the naval training ship in the foreground (*Radio Times/Hulton*)

105. (*opposite, below*) Donaghadee Harbour, Co. Down, and Copeland Island, in the 1880s (*Ulster Museum/R. J. Welch*)

106. Kingstown (Dun Laoghaire) showing the Mariners' Church, the Royal Marine Hotel, St. Michael's church, and the Town Hall, with the mailboat at its pier. Screw steamers were introduced in 1896, and the tower and spire of St. Michael's, here partially masked in scaffolding, were being completed in 1899 (*National Library*)

107. (*opposite, above*) Howth Harbour, Co. Dublin – the East pier in the late 1870s (*C. Flewitt*)

108. (*opposite, below*) River excursion, 1908. The paddle-steamer *Dartmouth Castle* ran from the railway at Youghal up the Blackwater to Cappoquin (*National Library*)

109. Paddling could be great fun . . . (*A. V. Henry*)

110. . . . so could lawn tennis, in 1893

FLYING PROFESSOR

111, 112. Professor George Francis FitzGerald of Trinity College, Dublin, was a serious scientist, F.R.S., pioneer of the electro-magnetic theory of radiation, but he took a practical interest in the idea of flight, so one autumn day in 1895 he tested his glider in College Park. A ramp was constructed for him to run down, and helpers to tow the glider like a kite; but though it flew splendidly by itself it would only carry him a few yards. However, here he is (*below*) with both feet clearly, if briefly, off the ground

113, 114. The occasion attracted curious spectators both inside and outside College Park, and the Professor took it seriously enough to remove his coat, though he retained his hat (*Jim Robson*)

ON THE RAILS

115. Or, occasionally, off them; the railways changed ways of life in Ireland from the 1830s onwards, but here is an exceptional event. A locomotive overshot the buffers at Harcourt Street Station, Dublin, on February 14, 1900. It stopped short of plunging into the street and was rescued, with difficulty, by road.

With the neglect of the railways in recent years, the Harcourt Street line is now closed (*Civic Museum/Old Dublin Society*)

116. The Lartigue Railway – a Victorian anticipation of the monorail. This odd-looking railway, with twin boilers for the locomotive and back-to-back carriages for the passengers, ran the nine miles from Listowel to Ballybunion in Co. Kerry from 1888 to 1924, when it was bought up by the regular railway and closed down (*National Library*)

117. (*opposite, above*) On the Kingstown line, the oldest in Ireland – the line from Dublin to Kingstown (Dun Laoghaire) was opened in 1834, and it is still open. This photograph was taken at Monkstown in the 1880s, but there is little change to be seen today (*National Library*)

118. (*opposite, below*) Victorian engineering on a Cyclopean scale – the Glinsk rail viaduct that carried the light railway from Killorglin to Valentia, Co. Kerry, from 1893. The line is now closed (*National Library*)

119. (*above*) The end of the line: Clifden station, about 1897, with the little train that connected Galway with Connemara. The line, opened in 1895, was closed in 1935 – one of the first lines in the country to go (*National Library*)

120. Horse-trams on College Green: from the 1870s to the 1940s, trams were a prominent figure of the Dublin scene. Here, about 1890, are the horse-trams, leisurely, uncrowded, outside the Bank of Ireland. In the foreground, Foley's statue of Henry Grattan; in the background, the ill-fated statue of William III, by Grinling Gibbons, which after many mutilations was finally blown up in 1929 (*National Library*)

121. Horse-trams mingle peacefully with sidecars and pedestrians opposite the West Front of Trinity College, ready to bring Dubliners to peaceful suburbs like Donnybrook and Drumcondra (*National Library*)

122. Steam tram to Lucan – St. James's Parish (Church of Ireland) Sunday School outing in 1895.
The Rev. J. C. Irwin and William Cunningham, the schoolmaster, are in the group in the foreground
(*Civic Museum/G. A. Henry*)

123. Electric trams at Sandymount Green, with its memories of James Joyce. Although it was at Sandycove that Joyce lived in his Martello Tower, Sandymount figures frequently in his writings, notably *Ulysses* and *Dubliners*. It has associations too with W. B. Yeats, a bust of whom stands in the Green, and it has changed little since their time. The shops shown in the photograph – Leverett and Frye on the left, Batt on the right – were still there a very few years ago.

Electric trams first appeared in Dublin in 1896, and the last route was not closed until 1949 (*National Library*)

124. One-horse tram at Warrenpoint; the tram ran between Warrenpoint and Rostrevor, Co. Down, from 1875 to 1915 (*Ulster Museum*)

125. At Dunluce Castle, Co. Antrim – a closed car and a 'toast-rack' in the 1890s (*National Library*)

126. The Donnybrook tram – a scene characteristic of Dublin in the Eighties and Nineties: top hats and billycocks, a soldier in his pill-box hat, and a Diorama showing in the Leinster Hall. Dioramas and Panoramas were among the many entertainments offered to city-dwellers before the coming of the big screen and little screen (*A. V. Henry*)

LEISURE

127, 128. The horse has always played a large part in Irish life and leisure, and the appearance of riders to hounds or in the show-ring changed only slowly over the years. Here are two generations: (*above*) Mr T. K. Laidlaw and Miss Laidlaw, of the Meath Hunt of 1911, with the young lady discreetly dressed for riding astride, and (*opposite left*) Mrs Stewart Duckett, riding side-saddle in 1877 (*Royal Dublin Society*)

129. (*opposite right*) A hero of 1868 – described as 'Shaun Rhue'

   Winner of the highest Stone Wall jump on record (6 ft 1½ in). Ridden by R. Flynn Esqre at Royal Dublin Society's Horse Show, 1868 held on the Lawn at Leinster House, the headquarters of the Society (*Royal Dublin Society*)

_ Shaun Rhue _

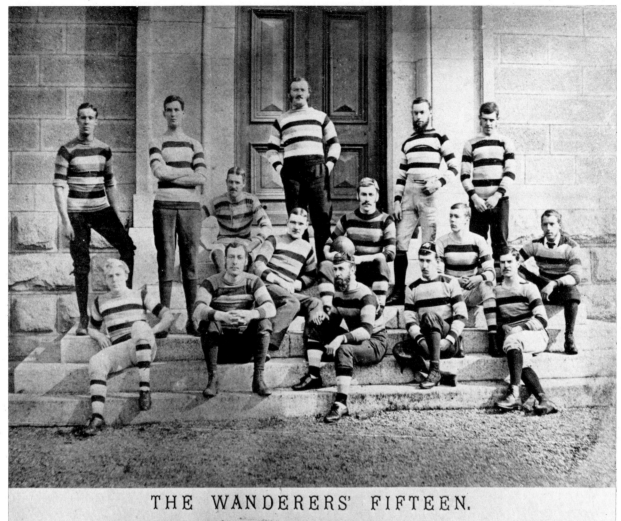

THE WANDERERS' FIFTEEN.

"CORK AND LIMERICK TOUR," &c., 1878-'79.

| F. MOORE | | D. F. MOORE | C. MANDERS | R. M. PETER | F. SCHUTE (Captain) | W. ROSS | W. NICHOLSON | C. C. WHITE |
| F. KENNEDY | | W. H. WALLIS | H. F. SPUNNER | H. L. ROBINSON | W. J. COULDING | F. W. BLOOD | W. KELLY |

130. Rugby football in the 1870s: Wanderers Football Club is more than a hundred years old, and its Dublin club-house has its walls lined with groups of past fifteens. Here is one of the earliest – the team that carried Dublin football into Munster in the season of 1878-79 (*Wanderers Football Club*)

131. Action picture of 1894: a line-out, with the ball in the air, during the final tie in the Leinster Cup of 1894, Wanderers v Trinity (Wanderers won). It will be seen that since 1878 Rugby players had become less chary of showing their bare knees (*Wanderers Football Club*)

132, 133. Hurlers of 1903: hurling, the fastest of field games, is also the oldest of all Irish games. It has been played in Ireland from the earliest recorded times, but it was first organised when the Gaelic Athletic Association was founded in 1884. (*Above*) The Senior Hurlers of Tullamore, Co. Offaly (or King's County, as it was then) in 1903 – or some of them; they played 17 a-side until 1913. (*Below*) the grass-roots foundation of the game is illustrated by this group of the hurlers of a parish at Tinnycross, near Tullamore, in 1900 (*G.A.A/Midland Tribune*)

134. *Pour le sport* – fashionably dressed for a shooting party in the Nineties
(*Mrs Wm. Jameson*)

135. (*above*) In spite of their petticoats, the little girls ran stoutly at the Guinness Show at Ballsbridge in 1904 (*Royal Dublin Society*)

136. (*below*) And the ladies enjoyed golf on the Lisfannon links at Buncrana, Co. Donegal (*National Library*)

WORK

137. Most of the people in Ireland worked on the land, but there were some big industries in the cities. W. & R. Jacob, Dublin biscuit manufacturers (and inventors of the cream cracker) showed a benevolent interest in their employees by running a sewing-class for girl workers, early in the twentieth century (*W. & R. Jacob and Co. Ltd.*)

138, 139, 140. Guinness has been brewed in Dublin since 1759 and it was already a large-scale industry when the photograph of the racking shed (*above*) was taken about 1890. Among the most skilled workers were the coopers on piece-work, the men who made the wood casks – the team of 1890 is seen opposite above; while the most pleasant part of the brewery was (and is) the Sample Room, seen opposite below about 1905 (*Guinness Museum*)

141, 142. Prize-winners: two fine horses and carters working for John Power's Dublin whiskey, prize-winners in the lorry tandem class in 1892; and (*below*) a prize-winning turn-out from the Mountjoy Brewery (one of Dublin's vanished breweries) in 1893 (*141, United Distillers of Ireland Ltd.; 142, Guinness Museum*)

143, 144. Linen-making and ship-building were the great industries in Belfast. Above, girls at work in a damask mill in York Street in 1890; below, workers leaving Harland and Wolff's shipyard in 1910 or 1911. The ship on the stocks in the background is the *Titanic* (*Ulster Museum*)

145, 146. There was plenty of small-scale industry, too, in town and country. (*Above*) back-street cobblers working under makeshift shelters in Dublin. (*Below*) A glass of poteen from an illicit still. Illicit distillation was widespread in many parts of Ireland. Poteen could be sold at a much lower price than 'Government whiskey', and making it was the only means by which many tenants could make up their rent money. So stills of this type abounded, especially in the wilder parts of the country, where they could more easily be hidden from the exciseman – though this group has the air of being arranged for the camera (*145, A. V. Henry; 146, F. E. Dixon*)

147. Tweed in the making, homespun and hand-woven. Making tweed was a cottage industry, especially in the North and West; here spinning, weaving and carding are on view in the weaving-shed attached to McKeown's Hotel at Leenane, Co. Galway, a tourist attraction for many years (*National Library*)

148, 149. Work of a different kind – one of the Gaelic League teachers, who travelled the country reviving the knowledge of Irish, taking a class of adults in the open air at Ballingeary, Co. Cork, in 1904 or 1905, and (*below*) a classroom in a regular school – Clash school in the parish of Athea, Co. Limerick, 1905 (*Kevin Danaher*)

FAMOUS OCCASIONS

150. O'Connell Centenary: great crowds turned out in Dublin in 1875 to celebrate the centenary of the birth of Daniel O'Connell, 'the Liberator'. Here is the scene at old Carlisle Bridge, looking up Sackville Street towards the Nelson Pillar and the portico of the General Post Office. At the corner on the left is Kelly's Fort, as it became known during the Easter Rising of 1916 (*Civic Museum/Old Dublin Society*)

151. Queen Victoria made four visits to Ireland during her reign. Here is a close shot of her on her last visit, to Dublin, in the spring of 1900, less than a year before she died

152. And here is a view of the crowds viewing the decorations in her honour in College Green (*Guinness Museum/Robert C. Booth*)

153. Unveiling Victoria: the memorial to Queen Victoria, seen here being unveiled in February 1908, stood in front of Leinster House, and stood there long after Leinster House had become the parliament building of a separate State. Unlike most royal statues in Dublin, it was never blown up and it was not removed until 1948. Victoria and her attendant figures, dismantled, are now resting in the courtyard of the former Royal Hospital, Kilmainham (*National Library*)

154, 155. Edward VII also visited Ireland several times, both as Prince of Wales and as king. Above is one of the triumphal arches erected in his honour – this one at Leeson Street Bridge in Dublin. On the right he is photographed, with Alexandra, in Kilkenny Castle, the seat of the Dukes of Ormonde (*154, F. E. Dixon; 155, National Library*)

156. No thronging crowds in this Dublin scene, though there is no mistaking Edward VII among the tall hats in the carriage (*G. A. Henry*)

157. He is equally unmistakable in this picture, but Kilkenny has turned out rather more of a crowd (*National Library*)

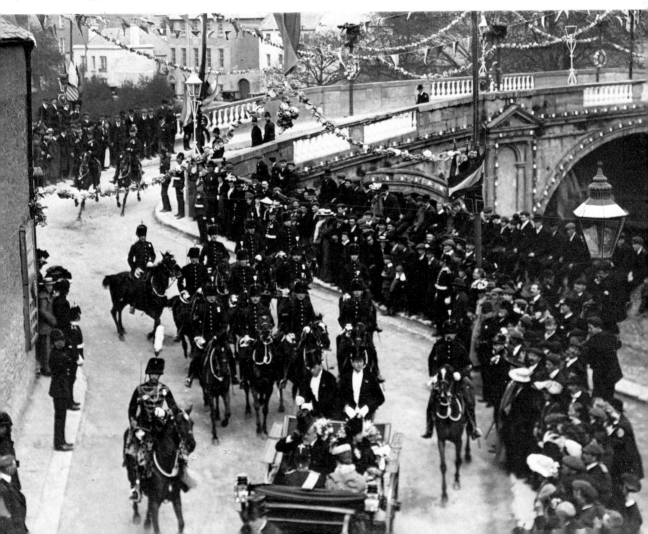

158, 159. Two great occasions in the fashionable world of Dublin – a Masonic Bazaar of 1882 in the Exhibition Hall in Earlsfort Terrace, built for the great exhibition of 1865, and (*left*) a Fancy Ball in Iveagh House, St. Stephen's Green, in 1880. Iveagh House, the town house of the Guinness family, has since been given to the nation by the Earl of Iveagh and now houses the Department of External Affairs (*Civic Museum/Old Dublin Society*)

160. In the two previous photographs the figures appear to be real enough, but the backgrounds seem to have been drawn in. In the photograph opposite, however, William England has got the complete scene at the original exhibition of 1865 – with hardly a move (*Radio Times/Hulton*)

THE DARKER SIDE

161. Felons of Our Land: Alongside the royal progresses and the fancy balls, there was suffering and revolt in Ireland all through the nineteenth century. Here are William Smith O'Brien (seated) and T. F. Meagher photographed in Kilmainham Jail after the failure of the rising of 1848. It all looks very friendly, with the soldier in attendance and the jailer holding his key, but the prisoners had both been sentenced to be hanged, drawn and quartered, and they were eventually transported for life.

Smith O'Brien was pardoned in 1854; 'Meagher of the Sword' escaped to America and took a prominent part on the Union side in the Civil War.

This is believed to be the first group photograph ever taken in prison. (*Mrs T. G. Moorhead*)

162. Eviction scene: all over Ireland people were constantly being turned out of their homes, either because they could not pay the rent (often an exorbitant rent) or because the landlord or his agent wanted to clear the estate of tenants. The battering-ram was used to break into barricaded houses and to wreck them so that they could not be lived in again (*National Library*)

163. Troops, police and bailiffs on eviction operations. (*Below*) preparing the battering-ram, whilst one of the bailiffs stands equipped not only with a crowbar but with a shield, in case the occupants of the beleaguered cottage try to defend themselves with boiling water (*National Library*)

164. (*opposite, above*) Mustering the forces – an eviction expedition ready to set off (*National Library*)

165. (*opposite, below*) Eviction completed – and the end of another humble home (*National Library*)

166. Mass without a church: where there was no church, Mass might be said in a *scalan*, a rough shelter, with the congregation in the open air. This congregation was photographed before Mass at Bunlin, Gortahork, Co. Donegal, in the 1860s. The priest can be seen standing in front of the *scalan* on the left (*Irish Folklore Commission*)

167. (*below*) Church without a roof: Mass in the roofless ruin of Ballintubber Abbey, Claremorris, Co. Mayo, also in the 1860s. The abbey, founded in 1216, was used for Mass all through penal times. It is now being restored (*Wynne, Castlebar/Bord Failte Eireann*)

168. Postscript to '48: William Smith O'Brien's daughter Lucy, married to
Dr John Gwynn, with two of her children. On the left, Stephen Gwynn (born
1864), afterwards well known as a writer and Irish Nationalist MP; on the
right, Lucy, who became the first Lady Registrar of Trinity College, Dublin
(*Mrs T. G. Moorhead*)

169. Prison walls: the domestic side of life in Kilmainham Jail, where many famous Irishmen were imprisoned and many died. The photograph above shows the Flewitt family, who were brought up in the prison – Thomas Flewitt photographed all the prisoners for record purposes in the days before fingerprints were used (C. Flewitt)

170. The grim interior of Kilmainham Jail in the 1860s. The Jail is now being restored by voluntary workers as a memorial to those who died there, including the leaders of the Easter Rising of 1916 (C. Flewitt)

171. (opposite) Curious onlookers at Newgate Prison in Green Street, the 'new Newgate' of 1773. It was on the iron balcony over the gate that condemned prisoners stood for public hangings; the fixture for the gallows can be seen above. This photograph was exhibited by W. J. Fitzpatrick, Esq., JP, of 49 Fitzwilliam Square, at the Irish Exhibition in London in 1888; the prison was demolished in the Eighties and the site is now a public park

AL FRESCO

172. Picnic at Killarney: the Irish Field Club in the woods beside the Upper Lake in July, 1898. An unconventional note, for the time, is struck by the man in the middle, who has not put his jacket on, even for the photograph (*Linenhall Library, Belfast*)

173. A smart turn-out of 1895; the coach and four, with its cargo of ladies in summer dresses, is standing outside Bangor Abbey, Co. Down (*Linenhall Library, Belfast*)

174. A quiet walk along the esplanade at Bray, Co. Wicklow, in 1895 – Bray Head in the background (*Radio Times/Hulton*)

175. A Jameson shooting party in 1893. The bearded figure on the right is the painter, Nathaniel Hone (*Mrs Wm. Jameson*)

176. And an *al fresco* lunch – the Jamesons again, with Miss Winslow from Boston on the right, and the manservant very correct, though as a concession to the surroundings he wears a cap (*Mrs Wm. Jameson*)

177. Ladies at leisure among the currachs at Kilkee, Co. Clare – a holiday resort in 1898 as it is today (*Radio Times/Hulton*)

178. Parish outing: St. Jude's Parish, Inchicore, ·went to Straffan, Co. Kildare, for their annual outing, travelling by barge up the Grand Canal

179. Swings were made on a handsome scale in 1893 (*Mrs Wm. Jameson*)

180. An open-air tea-party outside a farmhouse at Athea, Co. Limerick, about 1906 (*Kevin Danaher*)

181. All the fun of the fair at the Guinness Brewery Show at Ballsbridge, about 1904 (*Guinness Museum*)

182. A day out from Dalkey in 1901 or 1902: by train to Rathdrum, then by bicycle to Glendalough. Here, in the Vale of Clara, are (*from the left*) Victoria Booth, William Booth, 'Min' McKell, Edwin Booth, Ethel McComas (later Mrs Johnson of Foxrock), Nora Booth (later Mrs Forester-Paton of Alloa in Scotland, now in Australia) and Nellie McComas (later Mrs W. Wright of Carlow). The photographer was Robert C. Booth (*Guinness Museum/Robert C. Booth*)

183. The *Lough Neagh Queen* at Six Mile Water, Co. Antrim, in June 1904 (*Ulster Museum*)

184. Pause for lunch at the Upper Lake, Killarney – with a bugler to encourage the rowers in the most heavily laden boat (*National Library*)

185. Mysterious musicians – clearly something unusual in the way of open-air shows; but what kind of show it is, and where, remains a mystery – so far (*Dr W. E. Boles*)

ART AND LEARNING

186. Ireland's oldest university: Trinity College, Dublin, founded in 1591. This scene in Parliament Square was photographed by W. H. Fox Talbot in 1845 (*Science Museum*)

187. Pioneers: the first meeting of the Dublin Photographic Society, now the Photographic Society of Ireland, the second oldest in the world. This photograph, taken in 1854, was restored from a seemingly blank lantern slide by Harold White (*Harold White*)

188. Housewarming at St. Enda's. In 1910 Padraig Pearse moved his famous school, St. Enda's, from Cullenswood House to The Hermitage, Rathfarnham. This picture, from a negative found in Countess Markievicz's cottage, is believed to show the party he gave at the beginning of the autumn term, to celebrate the move.

Pearse himself is sitting at the end of the bench on the right, with Douglas Hyde, later President of Ireland (in the cap, looking left). Mrs Pearse, mother of Padraig and Willie, is next to Douglas Hyde; next to her, Professor Eoin MacNeill, later Chief of Staff of the Irish Volunteers. Standing under the window, behind the lady in a white hat, is Eamonn Ceant, who was shot with Pearse in 1916.

Others who may be identified are Fergus O'Kelly, George Plunkett and Colm O'Lochlainn, all at the end of the back row on the left; Desmond Ryan, under the window, without a hat; Micheal Mag Ruaidhri, the gardener, in a white hat, towards the end of the row; on his right, Frank Burke, who took over the school when it returned to Rathfarnham in 1920 and carried it on until 1935.

Also in the back row, to the right of Mag Ruaidhri, are Sean Dowling, Brian Joyce, and John MacDonagh, brother of Thomas, who was also shot in 1916

189. The Nine Graces, the newspapers called them – the first women to be admitted to degrees in the Royal University of Ireland. Their names were Emily Eberle, Marion Kelly, Louisa McIntosh, Isabella Mulvany, Alice Oldham, Annie M. Sands, Charlotte M. Taylor, Jessie Twemlow and Eliza Wilkins, but the only one who has been identified is Marion Kelly, standing on the far right of the back row. She was one of the five who took honours. The date was 1884

190. Students of the Seventies – the stewards at the college sports at Queen's College, Galway, in 1872 or 1873, photographed in the quad outside the windows of the Chemistry Lab. Their names, as recorded by J. J. Gorham, were; (*standing left to right*) '(Red)' Mark (McDonnell), W. Davis, Con Sloper, John Gordon, Rob O'Hara, Mat O'Callaghan, R. Glover, P. O'Kinealy (hidden by Dick Somerville's hat); (*sitting*) Sir A. Dempsey, Pitt Gorham, Jemmy Brodie, M. J. Moylan, Oswald Maiben, Mich White, Dick Somerville, J. J. Gorham; (*lying down*) Berny Clare, P. J. Prendergast. Most of these achieved distinction in after life – but most of them had to leave Ireland to do it

191, 192. When the British Association met in Dublin in 1878, the members went on an excursion to Parsonstown (Birr), to see the 6-foot telescope designed and built by the head of the Parsons family, the 3rd Earl of Rosse, who discovered the Spiral Nebulae. Then they were photographed on the steps of Birr Castle (*Royal Dublin Society*)

193. On stage at the old Abbey – and a centre of controversy. The history of Ireland's national theatre is studded with controversies. The first was over Synge's *Playboy of the Western World*, in 1907: the second over *The Shewing-Up of Blanco Posnet*, the first Shaw play to be done on its stage. It had been banned in England by the Lord Chamberlain; his writ did not run in Ireland, but Dublin Castle tried to stop the Abbey doing it. Lady Gregory and W. B. Yeats defied threats of withdrawal of their theatre's patent and fines of £300 a night, and the play went on in August 1909. Here is a scene from that historic production, with some of the most notable Abbey actors – Fred O'Donovan (on the table), Arthur Sinclair (sitting left), Maire O'Neill standing facing Fred, Sara Allgood standing far right (*Abbey Theatre*)

194. Veteran Scientist: Dr George Johnstone Stoney, F.R.S., mathematical physicist, who first introduced the word 'electron' into the vocabulary, was associated in turn with Trinity College, Dublin; Parsonstown Observatory; Queen's College, Galway; Queen's University; and the Royal Dublin Society, of which he was Secretary for 20 years and Vice-President for 30. Here he is in his laboratory at the Royal Dublin Society (*Royal Dublin Society*)

195. (*opposite*) Veteran Painter: Nathaniel Hone in his studio at Malahide, outside Dublin. Hone, the great-grand nephew of the eighteenth-century painter of the same name, worked in Paris for 17 years before returning to Ireland and settling in Malahide, where he lived from 1898 until his death in 1917 (*Mrs Wm. Jameson*)

ALL SORTS AND CONDITIONS

196. The Guard House at Roscrea, Co. Tipperary – a group photographed by Fox Talbot in 1853 (*Science Museum*)

197. Another Fox Talbot study of 1853: stonebreakers at Roscrea. The one on the right is wearing the traditional Irishman's costume, knee-breeches and tail-coat (*Science Museum*)

198. Dr J. A. Ray, the pharmacologist, and his son Armstedt, posed informally on the rocks at Bray Head (*Dr W. E. Boles*)

199. The Kerry Couple, in their traditional dress – the sort of picture that visitors to Ireland loved to take home (*F. E. Dixon*)

200. Portrait of a Victorian – photographer and sitter unknown (*G. A. Henry*)

201. Another informal pose – with the aid of a step-ladder. The people are (from the bottom) Mrs William Jameson (Henrietta Haig, sister of Douglas Haig), John Jameson, William Jameson (great-grandson of the original John Jameson, founder of the firm), James Penn, and Miss Winslow from Boston. The date was 1897 (*Mrs Wm. Jameson*)

202, 203. The Blackthorn Seller: on the left is the real photograph, on the right a coloured postcard version of it. The careworn, rather pathetic figure has been transformed into a bland, smiling character, his clothes tidied up, and the background converted into a picturesque rural scene. In such a fashion were many picture postcards made (*F. E. Dixon*)

204, 205. First Prizewinners of 1900, at the Royal Dublin Society's Spring Show at Ballsbridge. Ladysmith (*above*) was owned by Richard Green, of The Whittern, Kingston, Herefordshire. La Belle Charmante (*right*), calved April 19, 1898, was owned by Vere Ward Brown, of Balnagowan, Rathmines, Dublin, and bred by Fowler and de la Perrelle. Besides being first in her class she won the Rockgrave Challenge Cup, value £25 – so no wonder the elegantly-dressed lady with her looks proud (*Royal Dublin Society*)

206. Davy Stephens, the King of the Newsboys. For many years he sold his papers at Kingstown (Dun Laoghaire) where the mailboats come in; he was on chatting terms with crowned heads and other distinguished visitors; and every year he took the boat himself and crossed to Ascot, where he found many friends (*National Library*)